TREETURE CREATURES

AND

FLOWERBUDS

Published in the United Kingdom by:

Blue Falcon Publishing
The Mill, Pury Hill Business Park,
Alderton Road, Towcester
Northamptonshire
NN12 7LS
Email: books@bluefalconpublishing.co.uk
Web: www.bluefalconpublishing.co.uk

A CIP record of this book is available from the British Library.

First printed July 2021

ISBN 9781912765409

Use your pocket guide,
when you go outside.
Flowerbuds are at the back.
Take some snaps of who you track.
Share with us the ones you find,
To our buds and trees, be kind.

Good luck!

Bluebell

Bluebells

Myth: Bluebell woods are believed to be enchanted by fairies. It is thought these fairies set traps on those who visit.

They grow in woodland marking the start of spring.

Bluebells have sticky sap which was historically used to stick feathers to arrows

Daisy

Daisies

—

Myth: Daises are used for predictions of love. Many play the game "love me, love me not", taking a petal each time

They grow in meadows and gardens.

They close their petals at night when they are resting.

They are cheerful and bright and can be used to make Daisy Chains.

Buttercup

Buttercups

—

Myth: Hold a buttercup under your chin, if there is a yellow glow it is believed you like butter. However, the glow is due to the intense yellow shine which attracts insects.

They grow on most grassland.

They have 5 bright yellow petals.

Yellow Water-lily

Yellow Water-lily
—

It is the birth flower for the star sign Pisces.

They can be found in still or flowing fresh water.

They flower in the summer months and provide shelter for frogs.

Water lilies were made famous by French artist, Claude Monet

Dog-violet

Dog-violet

—

Dog-violet attracts fritillary butterflies to feed and lay eggs.

They can be found in woods, hedgerows and grassland.

They flower between April and June.

They are unscented.

Poppy

Poppies

—

They are a symbol of rememberance for those who died in the War.

They come in many colours, most popular is blood red.

Poppy oil is used as a salad dressing and cooking oil.

They flower between spring and summer.

Snowdrop

Snowdrops

—

Snowdrops are celebrated as a sign of Spring.

They are white bell-shaped flowers, found alongside rivers, in woodland and meadows.

They flower between January and February but sometimes as early as November.

Snowdrops are used as a pain killer for headaches and being tested for other medicinal uses.

Dandelion

Dandelions

—

Dandelions can be known as "wet the bed". Its roots have an ingredient that makes you need the toilet.

They evolved 30 million years ago.

The name in French means " Lions tooth", as they have sharp leaves.

They are used for food, medicine and dye.

Fruit is a hairy pappus which is referred to as a clock.

Forget-Me-Not

They are fragrant in the evening but not in the daytime.

They are the state flower of Alaska.

Found in woodlands and hedgerows.

They like shady spots under trees.

The
FLOWER
TRAIL

Did you see me?

Buttercup

Daisy

Bluebell

Yellow
Water-lily

Snowdrop

Poppy

Dandelion

Forget-me-not

Dog-viole

Wild flowers have many benefits, this is due to the fact they support declining bee populations. Bees and other insects pollinate our wild flowers, which is vital for our eco-system.

Treeture Creatures and Flowerbuds
Book 1 – Oaky the Oak Leaf

illustrated by
Gaynor Volpi

Oaky
the
Oak Leaf

Marian Hawkins

In this story, we follow Oaky the oak leaf on his exciting adventure as he tries to make his way back home and meets some unfamiliar characters on the way!

Available to buy from Amazon, Waterstones and Foyles.

Treeture Creatures and Flowerbuds
Book 2 – Willow the Willow Leaf

illustrated by
Gaynor Volpi

Willow
the
Willow Leaf

Marian Hawkins

t's Willow's turn for an adventure this time, as the little
af finds himself washed downstream and makes many new
ends as he tries to find his way back to where he belongs.

Available to buy from Amazon, Waterstones and Foyles.

Treeture Creatures and Flowerbuds
Book 3 – Beech the Beech Leaf

When an unsuspecting beech leaf is whisked away on a ba
she learns a lot about the trees and flowers that surroun
her as she bounces, floats and squelches her way back t
her beloved beech tree!

Available to buy from Amazon, Waterstones and Foyles.

Notes

_____

_____

_____

_____

_____

_____

_____

_____

_____

_____

_____

_____

_____

_____

_____

_____

_____

_____

9 781912 765409